T0197384

THE MIND OF AN
(ALMOST)
Typical Girl

GRACE BROWN

AuthorHouse™
1663 Liberty Drive
Bloomington, IN 47403
www.authorhouse.com
Phone: 1 (800) 839-8640

Published by AuthorHouse 03/28/2019

ISBN: 978-1-7283-0022-1 (sc)
ISBN: 978-1-7283-0023-8 (e)

authorHOUSE®

"We of the craft are all crazy."
~Lord Byron

Preface

I want to start by confessing that I am not publishing this book under my full legal name. Grace is my name, but not all of it. It is not that I am ashamed of who I am. I am proud of how I live with OCD and mild autism and anxiety. What I am not proud of is how people treat other people with these disorders. I love this cause, but I am not ready to be a martyr for it. I think that the best thing I can do for myself and other mentally ill people is live a normal life and writing under this name allows me to do that.

I have many reason for writing a book like this, or rather collecting the materials to publish it. Among them are the fulfillment of a childhood dream to be a published author, but that's not the main reason I decided to write *this* book at *this* time. I've been through a lot in my life, but the hardest part of everything was always how alone I felt and how hard I found it to explain how I was feeling. It took me years, my whole life really, to be able to talk about things in the way I do now.

I understand more than most people that years can be too long to wait for understanding. I hope that, by writing this book, people will have something to point at and say "this is how I feel" or "read this if you want to understand." I never had that. There wasn't that piece of material for me to point to so I began writing my own. I wanted to be able to tell people how situations felt to me. I worked very hard and poured over metaphors, some seen more than once in the course of the book, to explain different feelings. I made my own material.

When you read this, please try to forget that I have bad OCD and that I'm very mildly autistic and that I suffer from anxiety. When you read this, please try to see me as a person. Just another person. Please try to relate to me as a person, not a person who has OCD or autism or anxiety. That's where I believe true understanding will begin.

I am a Creative Girl
(Written at age 11)

I am a creative girl who loves to write
I wonder if I will ever reach my goal
I hear words fly off the page
I see much more than a bunch of letters
I want to show the world what I see
I am a creative girl to loves to write

I pretend I am a real writer
I feel a rush of crazy ideas
I touch their hearts, or at least I try
I worry about my grades
I cry when it doesn't turn out right
I am a creative girl who loves to write

I understand that the chances of me succeeding are slim
I say I'll try anyway
I dream of complete and total success
I try as hard as I possibly can
I hope that that is enough
I am a creative girl who loves to write

Speechless
(Written at age 13)

Walking to the grave,
Happiness stolen away,
This moment he saves,
Though the child has nothing to say.

With eye's teary gloss,
Downward he kneels,
In sadness' bitter frost,
As a young heart heals.

Although he remembers not,
Love, in his heart he bears,
Deep in mourning thought,
For memories were shared.

So young, in his wisdom,
So depressed in his sorrow,
Once he leaves, we come,
A tearful glance, we borrow.

Seek

(Written at age 16)

The biggest battles we wage,
Are behind a closed door,
And in it's worse stage,
We need friends all the more.

Then we put our armor on,
And try to stand up tall,
But it's all just a con,
Because we feel so small.

We push all our friends away,
So they won't see us like this,
Trying to keep emotions at bay,
But our intentions go amiss.

Sometimes we have to fall apart,
So we can pull ourselves together,
We know deep in our hearts,
It's a storm we have to weather.

After all, to be truly strong,
We mustn't be afraid to be weak,
It's a battle that can be life-long,
If it's true happiness we seek.

I Find Myself Questioning
(Written at age 16)

I find myself questioning my mortality.
And how could I not?
When everything you hear on the news is a tragedy.
And we are huddled in the corner,
Trying to make sense of the senseless,
Or else ignore it all completely,
Because it's all just too much to handle.
With death pouring in all around me,
How could I not question my mortality?

I find myself questioning my sanity.
And how could I not?
When a flood of emotions keep on washing over me.
And I'm lying in my bed at night,
Just trying to breathe.
And I'm not sure if people feel these things like me,
Or if I'm just alone in my struggles.
With my heart about to burst out of my chest,
How could I not question my sanity?

I find myself questioning my ability.
And how could I not?
When all of this judgment keeps coming at me?
And I'm graded and scored everywhere I go,
Trying my best to be good enough.
And people say it's all to make me better,
But it just overwhelms me.
With so many prying eyes staring at me,
How could I not question my ability?

I find myself questioning me.
And how could I not?
When I'm still figuring out who I'm going to be.
And my future's out there at my feet,
And I feel like there's nothing I can't be.
I feel like I have unlimited potential,
And I can be anything I want to be.
With my whole life ahead of me,
How could I not question me?

Thoughts on Death
(Written at age 16)

Death has a certain finality
It is not true when they say
That memories can keep them alive
It is true
That memories will fade
It is foolish to think
That the pain will fade and memories will remain
You need to know
Over time things won't get better
It may seem like
People get over it
But they never do
Some people think that things stay the same
They are right
Some people think that we must be optimistic
That is unrealistic
We must get over it
Some people believe
It is just the way it is
I disagree
(read backwards)

The OCD Poem
(Written at age 17)

Every stanza has four lines,
And there are four stanzas, no more,
Make sure every line rhymes,
With the line two before.

You get an idea in your head,
And you can't get it out.
You just lie there in bed,
And this one thought seems to shout.

Dream about it when you sleep,
Think about it incessantly,
And in your subconscious you keep,
The thought going constantly.

It's done, what then?
Make sure it's how it should be
Read it again. Read it again. Read it again.
This is OCD.

Sometimes It's an Ocean
(Written at age 18)

I'm in an ocean of water but there's nothing to drink. I'm drowning and dehydrated in the same breath and the thing that I reach for is the very thing that's tearing me apart inside. And I take my meds **day after day after day after day after day after day after day after day** but it doesn't stop the song that's stuck in my head. It just turns down the volume and I don't know if I want it switched off. I don't know if I can deal with the silence. And I try to play it but I've never been a very good musician and I never get the tune right and people try to sing along but they don't know the words and I have to come to grips with the fact that I'm hearing it alone. And it's the best song ever sung and I don't want anyone else to ever hear it and I don't know if I'm doing it for them or me. Things get **stuck stuck stuck stuck stuck stuck stuck stuck** in my head and it takes a chisel to get it out and the chisel is made of eights and shapes and locking my car. **Open four times lock eight times open four times lock eight times open four times lock eight times open four times lock eight times open four times lock eight times open four times lock eight times open four times lock eight times open four times lock eight times.** **And I fight and I fight and I fight and I fight and**

I fight and I fight and I fight. And I claw my way through and then finally! **Open two times lock four times open two times lock four times open two times lock four times open two times lock four times**.

And that's all I can do and it seems to be as big as a grain of sand, but for me it's the entire shore. And I stand for a moment and enjoy the sun, but the tide is coming in. And I **breathe breathe breathe breathe breathe breathe breathe breathe** before it pulls me in again. And my throat still burns because I didn't have time to get a drink on shore but right now I'm just focused on getting up for air. And someone from a boat calls "learn how to swim." And I'm terrified that someone saw me drowning and I held my breath and said those three little letters. They smile. "Me too." And I imagine the waves crashing into the front of their skull and think maybe someone is hearing the same song as me but it's always a different melody. Or there's no song at all. Why do they want to live in a storm when their stream barely has a current? They still say that **they are they are they are they are they are they are they are they are**. I didn't know it was something that you could be. But maybe I missed that lesson at school because I was counting eights on the clock or doing triangles in my notebook or in the bathroom trying not to be sick because I forgot how many times I locked my car. **Open two lock four open two lock four open two lock four open two lock four**.

I don't like the number between twelve and fourteen. I like squares and right triangles. I want the volume at an even number. I need the thermostat at a five. I count the tiles on the ceiling. I don't let my food touch on my plate. I like the number eight. I love the number eight. I **love love love love love love love love** the number eight. I take my meds **every day every day every day every day every day every day every day every day**. I take it just to try to be okay, but sometimes I feel like I'm **miles away miles away miles away miles away miles away miles away miles away miles away**. People tell me to just stop. To stop. If I could stop, I would **stop stop stop stop stop stop stop stop**. But I can't make the music go away.

The most beautiful song to ever be sung lives in my head and I want to play it for everyone and I don't want anyone to ever have to **hear it again hear it again hear it again hear it again hear it again hear it again hear it again hear it again**. People don't think it's playing because they can't hear it too. Like, somehow, if I can't show them, it can't be true. Eight tons of pressure resting on my shoulders and they want to sit on top of them? They think **it's not true not true not true not true not true not true not true not true**. It makes me want to go back into my head **shut the door shut the door shut the door shut the door shut the door shut the door shut the door shut the door** and lock it. **Open two lock four open two lock four open two lock four open two lock four.**

I Don't Know

(Written at age 18)

I don't know if it's starting or ending.
I don't know what it is.
All I know is my world is bending,
And reality's starting to fizz.

I don't know what to do,
If anything at all.
It's all still very new,
And I don't know if I'll rise or fall.

I don't know where I'm going,
Or from where I came,
And though I have no way of knowing,
I know I'll never be the same.

From an Obsessive Mind

(Written at age 18)

One, two, three, four,
Five, six, seven, eight,
I'll count some more,
I just might be late.

Hip hop, hippity hop,
Music volume at five,
Or else my ears will pop,
Multiples of five just jive.

Click, click, clickity click,
Unlock my car four times,
The number seems to stick,
In my head it just chimes.

Slowly, careful, straight,
Steady hand, good line,
Doesn't matter the rate,
If it's straight it'll be fine.

Right angles and squares,
Triangles and 45 degrees,
Are the perfect pairs,
Just put my mind at ease.

Plates with little sections,
Make sense in my head,
All these little bargains,
I make to go to bed.

Numbers and geometry,
Evenness and lines,
Makes things easier to see,
Like little perfect signs.

To make this poem perfect,
To finish what I create,
I need just one more set,
To make the stanzas eight.

Who I Am

(Written at age 18)

As I sit here writing about who I think I am, I can't help but think back to a few days ago. I was sitting on a leather couch talking about acronyms that describe me with a man who has quite a few acronyms after his own name. Obsessive-compulsive disorder. Generalized anxiety disorder. Autism spectrum disorder. OCD, GAD, ASD. It's not hard to imagine these combinations of letters defining a person. There are a lot of things that change with these letters. While most people take medications to combat headaches or shorten their flu symptoms, I take them every day. With names like fluoxetine, lamotrigine, and alprazolam, it can be daunting.

Every day I take two medications that change the chemical composition of my brain. One increases the amount of serotonin left in my brain. The other increases the amount of dopamine. I'd be lying if I said that this didn't make me pause and wonder if I am the same person I was a couple of months ago. The truth is, I'm really not. In the months since 2016, I've had quite the ride. Two trips to the emergency room for crisis care after self-harm incidents. The first trip came with the decision to change psychologists. A new psychologist, my first psychiatrist, and my first dose of medication; ten milligrams of fluoxetine. I fielded a wide range of side effects; headaches, stomachaches, loss of focus, hyper focus, and of course, the "pleasant" sensation of uncontrolled shaking.

I had always fancied myself an intelligent human being. I spent my middle school years in the gifted program and honors classes and my high school years balancing honors and AP classes. All of a sudden, I was failing two classes. Two classes that I liked, classes that I was supposed to be good at. As I hid my new insecurities behind my favorite SAT words, I wondered again if I was the same person now. If I was, I certainly didn't feel like it. I was admitted to College with a considerable scholarship and wondered if I would be able to keep it. I continued to go through weekly sessions with my psychologist and monthly sessions with the psychiatrist. Ever changing doses of medication and pills growing in size kept me occupied.

So now I will return to the topic of this essay who am I? The truth is, I'm not sure that I know. I'm not the same person that I was at the beginning of this year. I'm not the same person that I was last month and last week and even yesterday. My sense of self is changing constantly, and it's not just because of the alphabet soup of diagnoses that now threaten to describe me. It's because I'm eighteen years old. Well, to be exact, I'm eighteen years, six months, and four days old, in counting. If anyone tells you that they know exactly who they are, they are sadly mistaken. I'm still finding out who I am and who I want to be.

Who am I right now? At eighteen years, six months, and four days old, who am I? I'd like to believe I'm an intelligent young woman. My mind isn't exactly like your mind or anybody else's and I love it. Every day I gain more insight into who I am as a person. Once a week, before I go to bed, I take an inventory of my character. I introduce Grace to myself. I start, "My name is Grace and I am fourteen, fifteen, sixteen, seventeen, eighteen years old." I try to think of how I presented myself to the world that week and how I thought about myself in my own head. I think about the things that I can improve on and the things I am happy with.

The biggest inspiration for my introspective process of character inventory is my family, my biggest source of character. I grew up around people who talked in big words and loved with big hearts. At three years old, my favorite word was precisely and my best friend was my cousin. I gave hugs, I talked to everyone, I wandered around the stage at my first dance recital. That was who I was. I was like everyone else in my family and it was safe. I'm not exactly like one member of my family anymore. I try to be the best parts of all of them to be myself.

I don't always have the easiest time with people. I'm social and talkative and, most of the time, happy, but that doesn't lessen my social isolation. I don't use words that most people use. My favorite book is *The Scarlet Letter*. I'm an old soul. At the same time, I don't understand tone all of the time. I struggle with sarcasm and jokes that cause me to have different relationships with my fellow students. I'm not normal, but who would ever want to be normal? I am exactly who I am and I might not know exactly who that is yet, but I'm figuring it out.

My Thanksgiving in a Mental Hospital

(Written at age 19)

I just spent a week in a psychiatric ward. I never saw myself in this kind of situation. I didn't know how this could happen because I had the "perfect" parents, the "perfect" family, the "perfect" life. No one told my obsessive compulsive disorder that.

It got way beyond the quirkiness people think it is, and that's how I ended up giving up all of my privacy for seven days. It was nothing like we expected, but at the same time, exactly how you thought it would be. People's shoes are held together by a little Velcro strap because there were no strings on the psych ward, even shoelaces. I painted with watercolors and did puzzles and sat in circles talking about how much I liked triangles. I did not, however, wear a hospital gown and walk around like an over-medicated zombie. I wore yoga pants every day because they were comfortable and still made me feel presentable. I wore sweaters and cute little shirts with cardigans. When I did wear shoes, they were cute little brown ankle boots.

The ward is the only place I've ever been where you could openly ask someone what they were diagnosed with, which normalized everything that was going on in my head. The assumption on the ward was that you had attempted suicide at least once, but no one judged you for that. The idea of going to the hospital was one of the scariest thoughts imaginable. I was in college and had to leave before the semester was over without knowing if I could get any credit for the classes I had worked so hard in. I was completely cut off from the outside world. For a few hours a day, you could make calls on phones mounted on the wall — no privacy. There were visiting hours twice a day and at least one of my parents came to everyone, bringing food because I was a picky eater. Near the end, it was really hard to see my parents leave when I had to stay. I wanted desperately to go home on Wednesday, or even Thursday morning, and be home for Thanksgiving. I wasn't.

I absolutely love Thanksgiving, but not for the food. I eat very few of the "traditional" Thanksgiving foods so that isn't why it is so special. I wanted to be with family all day and play games and laugh and eat different pies for hours. I had to settle for a small meeting room at the hospital. My mom brought a Thanksgiving-themed table cloth, napkins, cups, even a pie she'd made. I ate turkey and this sweet potato thing that I absolutely love. My aunt sent me some brie cheese and this grilled bread and balsamic vinegar things to eat it with (she knows the way to my heart). I felt so loved. A friend I had made while in-patient didn't have any family there to celebrate with her — so I asked her if she would like to eat with me and my parents. It was a super simple Thanksgiving, we didn't even have mashed potatoes, but she was really happy to eat it with us. Her prayer before we ate will always stick with me, no matter how old I get. She thanked God for the family she didn't know she had. We had a great time; the stories of my friend's life were amazing. After pumpkin pie, we played a game, Taboo to be exact.

You would probably be surprised by all the laughter in our little psych ward, but, as I had said before, psychiatric hospitals are nothing like you would expect. I think I went to sleep at like 8 p.m. because turkey makes you so tired, but that day was the best Thanksgiving I've ever had. The next day, I was discharged back to the outside world, but I will never forget that Thanksgiving.

What it's like
(Written at age 19)

Do you know when you were little and you'd have bad dreams? Not the ones that you normally have, the kind you have when you're really sick. The Tim-Burton-esque nightmares that make no sense. It's like having a small part of your brain that filters everything through that nightmarish lens and then your mind is running all your thoughts through there until your only break is when you're asleep. Then the nightmares are about waking up.

It's like there's a song stuck in my head. It's the most beautiful song that's ever been sung and I want to share it and keep it for myself at the same time. No matter how many times I try to play it, nobody ever gets the beat right. Nobody can learn the lyrics. I try and I try until I have to come to grips with the fact that I'm listening alone. Beautiful agony in my mind. The meds come in to turn down the volume, but never turn it off. I don't want them to because, without the music, I don't know who I am.

It's like being thrown into the sea thirsty. The thing you need the most is the very thing threatening to kill you. Your desires for air and water fight each other, but, despite being surrounded by both, you'll never have either. It's like bobbing up and down with your throat burning and your muscles aching. Then a boat passes by. They say "Learn to swim. We did."

Empathy
(Written at age 20)

The pain isn't mine to feel.
The heart isn't mine to break.
I always seem to steal,
The pain of another's mistake.

It comes ripping through,
From their mouth to my soul.
But what can I really do,
To fill this brand new hole?

The air runs out of my chest.
I don't know where it goes.
Maybe it's all for the best.
But no one ever really knows.

The tears aren't mine to shed.
The guilt isn't mine to bear.
Yet, deep inside my head,
It all remains buried there.

Choices

(Written at age 20)

I lost a lot of my choices to the alphabet soup
that tries to become who I am
so I convince myself that I would have made the decisions
taken away from me regardless
and I keep tucked away in the recesses of my mind
a version of me with no diagnoses
so I can tell myself that who I am is not a product of acronyms
filed away in some doctor's cabinet
and in reality I've made these choices
and they haven't made me I can list off the cons of any number of things I can't do
and I talk about how great it is living alone because I know
I'm not built to live around other people
and I convince everyone that everything is exactly how I want it to be
so they won't see that in reality I'm lonely
and I'm painfully aware of all the amazing parts of living with people around you
but try my best not to think about what can never happen
and the friends I've made live typical lives
and wonder why I exclude myself from conversations
when really I'm protecting myself from places I can never go and things I can never do
and the hope that comes with making these plans
that always end in disappointment or disaster
and I fall back into my alphabet soup
and everything I do everything I say is carefully crafted
to keep my head above the surface
and all the thought that it requires leaves me exhausted even when I don't say a word
and I know breaks are important for me but it doesn't make them any less lonely
because it's not about sitting with yourself and being comfortable with who you are
it's about knowing everyone is together and you're trapped in place

just as much as if the door was locked barricaded in
by symptoms you can't control that don't align at all with who you actually are
so you take pills to be more yourself
all the while trying not to lose yourself
and you wonder if maybe the alphabet soup is who you were all along
and you wonder if you traded who you are for a chance at a normal life you'll never have
and come to grips with your dependency on little pills in time to wake up to
a life you have to work so hard to love.

To my OCD brain
(Written at age 20)

Hello? Can you hear me back there?
We both know I can hear you
You're just about everywhere
There's really nothing I can do

I always listen to what you say
Though rarely follow your advice
If the communication went the other way
Well I've always thought that'd be nice

I really don't know what I'm doing
Hoped it'd find its way along
I usually go through poetry like others sing
But maybe you were writing the song

How much of you am I?
How short is the fuse?

How tight is this tie?
How much do I have to lose?

I take things into myself
To try and kick you out
All for the sake of my health
It's not you, but me that it's about

It doesn't work, not all the way
Does that make you glad?
I actually am, I have to say
The silence would drive me mad

Have I hurt your feelings?
Do you even have feelings at all?
I haven't forgotten the good things
The bad things just stack up so tall

The Battle
(Written at age 20)

We are fighting a losing battle
Never will it be said that
We have control of our lives
We have to look and see that
The powerful and wealthy rule the world
It's ridiculous for us to think
Our voices matter and should be heard
We're meant to feel hopeless but
People are still fighting against it
They're fools, wasting their time
The powerful will push back
There's nothing more powerful than determination

People march all over the country
People stand for what they believe in
They don't know what I know that
The powerful feel they've already won
It's not enough that
We are trying our hardest
We must accept
They're the strongest
It'd be dumb to think
We're stronger
(read in reverse)

A Moment in My Life
(Written at age 20)

My dad had gotten me from school, picked up my mom, and drove straight to the emergency room. Nobody even woke me up when we got there and the next thing I knew we were at the ER. I don't remember much of being there. For the most part I was out of tears, but occasionally I'd get myself pulled together enough to cry for a couple minutes. When we got to the hospital it was just a big old-fashioned house in the dark. I was dead on my feet, basically sleepwalking through rooms with off-brand kids' shows playing in the background.

I don't even know when they took a picture of me, but I saw it later on my intake forms so I know that it happened. A very tall, very slim man appeared after what might have been a minute or an hour. He was covered in shadows from the pitch black night and I have no real recollection of what he looked like. He led us around what felt like some sort of maze with concrete sidewalks and big black buildings. The further we went in the more I knew that I'd never find my way out. We finally stopped at a building that was completely indistinguishable from the rest, but this was the one I was going to live in.

The walls were so white and the florescent lights so harsh that everything around me seemed to glow an unnatural neon blue. It was dead silent except for a woman snoring down the hall. My parents stayed with me to fill out paperwork even though I was technically an adult, but they left soon after. Next up, a strip search. I was freezing cold and completely exposed while I stood in another harshly lit room with two women. One was calling out identifying marks. "Two tattoos, scars on her shoulders and one on her left knee, a lot of back acne," I thought that last one was a bit harsh. I didn't get any of my stuff back that night. They showed me to a room with a sleeping woman on the other side and I slept in my clothes. The clothes on my back and the rock I'd been holding for probably close to twelve hours now felt like the only things I had in this world. I was officially admitted to a mental hospital.

My first night on the ward I slid all over the place. I couldn't keep myself in one spot, despite being in a twin sized bed almost too small to roll over in. I felt like I was falling out. Out of my mind, out of my family, out of my life, but mostly out of my bed. I didn't exactly expect to sleep well that night and I assumed there would be some fancy word for how what had happened the day before had caused me to feel this way. I was wrong. The real answer was very simple: in a mental hospital there are no fitted sheets. I was sliding off the bed because my sheets were.

The ward felt like a planet close enough to earth to make you forget you're somewhere else between all the little things that remind you it wasn't like where you were before at all. My particular ward was called STAT, which stood for Short Term Assessment and Treatment. This meant that nobody on the ward was living there. The longest you could stay on a STAT ward was two months. I couldn't brush my teeth that morning because I hadn't gotten all of my belongings back, but I did go into the bathroom. Another thing about a psych ward: there are no bathroom doors. There was a curtain, sort of like a very long shower curtain, that went from floor to ceiling across an opening in the wall that was much wider than a door. Like many things, I found this made sense in theory, but was still very strange to see in practice.

When I finally got back my belongings they weren't in the bags that I had packed them in because, third shocker of the day, there were no zippers on the ward. Instead I woke up to a brown paper bag and an old plastic laundry basket. They had refolded all my clothes for me when they were done looking through them. I think about that sometimes. They were going through a complete stranger's clothes in the middle of the night and, when they were done, they had folded them again.

I met my roommate Lauren that morning who was also experiencing her first hospitalization. I thought we seemed about the same age, but she was actually twenty-nine. We didn't talk for very long, but I could tell that Lauren's life was being ruined by her mental illness. She told me how she was committed last night and would lose her job because she didn't have any more days to take off. She said how, on one income, she and her husband would not be able to afford their dream house, which they just bought, and they would have to move in with her parents. Even though there were stark differences in our diagnoses, I saw something that I feared for myself in Lauren.

I went out to the day room for the first time to eat breakfast and noticed almost immediately that the average age in the room was about fifty. I sat down next to a woman who appeared to be in her seventies and began to talk to her. Her name was Valerie and it was definitely not the first time that she had been hospitalized. She reminded me of a grandmother, old, a little frail, very sweet, but she was a grandmother who had been regularly trying to kill herself for longer than I'd been alive. That was her main diagnosis: depression. I told her about mine, severe obsessive-compulsive disorder. This was when I had my first experience with conversations about my hands.

Anyone who is around the mental health community and has seen people with severe enough OCD to land them in the hospital knows that they are, without fail, hand washers. A hallmark of severe OCD is hands that are dry, cracked, and often bleeding. I, however, am not a hand washer. I've had a few experiences where I washed my hands a couple dozen times, but I overall have no issue with this. I personally think that my hands are stunningly normal, even a little deformed. I have long fingers, but they're crocked and besides that I just think that my hands are too big for my wrists.

Valerie didn't think so. She immediately commented on my hands, how smooth they were, how soft and pretty they looked. Not only that, she wanted to touch my hands. To feel the hands of someone with OCD who wasn't a hand washer. It was probably one of the oddest experiences of my life up until that point. It turned out to be something that I had to get used to, though, because it wouldn't be the last time I heard comments about my hands. To this day, when I'm in the mental health community, I field questions and compliments about my hands.

I had watched TV shows and movies about mental hospitals so I expected a nurse to come to give me my meds that morning, I hadn't taken any the night before, on a little tray and check my mouth when I was done, but no one there was my servant. There was nothing physically wrong with me or any of the other patients on the ward so I don't know why I thought they would cater to us. Right up by the front desk was the meds window, which would open up three times a day with a nurse handing out everyone's medications. When the window opened, you went and stood in line. If you didn't get in line someone would call you from the hallway to come over, but no one was bringing you your meds.

The first person to seek me out was a girl named Claire. She was eighteen and one of the few younger people on the ward so it made sense that we would talk. This was definitely not Claire's first hospitalization. She had been in and out of hospitals since her early teens and, by this point, her parents didn't seem to be in the picture anymore. Claire had a complicated diagnosis that included borderline personality disorder, depression, bipolar disorder, and anxiety. I found it very hard to follow her train of thought most of the time, but one thing that she made very clear was that she could talk to birds and see and communicate with dead people who, for some reason, were all over the ward.

Claire didn't want us to tell any of the nurses about her supernatural abilities because she thought they would put her on antipsychotic drugs. She talked a lot about getting out of the hospital and smoking weed, which made Valerie very angry. Valerie asked her several times why she was there getting help at all if she was just going to throw it away as soon as she got out, but Claire didn't seem too bothered by this. She was released just a few days after I was admitted. I later found out that she had some sort of break from reality and was involuntarily committed to a hospital in Delaware a few days after she left. Sometimes I wonder what would have happened if the nurses knew about her other "abilities."

Everyone had a social worker and mine was named Sarah or Cara or something like that. She was friendly, but in a way that could've been sincere or just completely fake. There were doctors and psychiatric nurses and therapists so this Sarah or whoever she was seemed like the least qualified person to spill my guts to. She was mainly there for legal reasons, as I understood it, but she seemed to be waiting for me to break down. I spoke to her more formally and spoke emotionally in therapy, which I thought was very appropriate. In the end, she delayed my release two days because she said I hadn't emotionally processed what had happened. I didn't realize I had to cry in front of every hospital employee to be seen as stable.

Something that I had to learn fast if I was going to get anything out of this experience was that my peer group had changed. Most of the people that I was receiving treatment with were closer to my parents' age than mine and, while I treated them with respect, I couldn't treat them as my elders. A big part of group therapy is input and even advice from the group, but it seemed very odd to be giving advice to people who were twice or even three times my age. Beyond that, it wasn't like my life was going that great at the moment. I don't think I said a word about myself or anyone else in my first group therapy session. I just listened.

Getting better in a mental hospital meant that I had to speak during group therapy. I got great advice from the therapist, but I also learned a lot in my failed attempts to give advice from time to time. I learned some of the ways I coped didn't actually work and some of my beliefs didn't make sense. Other patients would ask me, point blank, why I felt the way I did and sometimes that was the first chance I'd had to think about it. Those things I never thought about were suddenly the only things I had to worry about. Everything else was taken care of for me: my food, my meds, my schedule, where I slept. It was a huge relief to be able to give all that responsibility to someone else and that's what let me get better.

Some of the conversations I found myself in weren't ones I ever thought would happen at all. I listened to Valerie, my grandmotherly figure, talk about how she longed to go home and be intimate with her husband again. How was I supposed to have any advice or input about that at nineteen? A woman talked about the difficulties of raising a kid my age and looked to me to say something about it, but I couldn't find anything to say. I had an increasing feeling that I had no right to be there. Not that I didn't belong there because I most certainly needed hospitalization, but that I had no right to be struggling like I was.

I heard stories of people who went through lifetimes of pain and abuse before developing the symptoms that I had. I heard about siblings dying at heartbreakingly young ages and families no longer wanting anything to do with their mentally ill loved ones. I heard about rejection on the basis of sexuality and personality alike. I heard about a boy my age whose father didn't want him to come home and yet one of my parents visited me twice a day. My dad drove five hours round trip so I could be in a hospital near home. My family brought me pictures and my close friends would call me whenever the phones were on, which was a limited amount of time during the day. Sometimes, listening to these stories of a lifetime of heartache and loss, I felt as though I had no right to be as severely mentally ill as I was. With such a great family and a great life, I had no legitimate reason to be. Despite the support of all the professionals and patients around me, I still struggle with that feeling today.

One of the people I befriended at the hospital was Adam. Adam was eighteen years old, less than a year younger than me and the closest to my age after Claire left. Adam and I were similar in a lot of ways. It was our first hospitalization, we were both fairly bright, and we could both pass pretty easily as not having any mental illness at all. To this day, I don't know Adam's diagnosis. We became friends over one of the most cliché psych ward activities: a puzzle. This was a thousand-piece puzzle that seemed relatively untouched so there was a good chance that all the pieces were still there.

Adam and I shared another thing in common: the ability to hyper focus. We could sit and do the puzzle for hours without getting bored and taking very few breaks. Months later I would try to do a similar puzzle, but didn't find it nearly as interesting as it was in the hospital. We didn't talk very much, but I still considered us friends at that point. Slowly, I learned more about Adam. He was the only one on the ward who had been involuntarily committed. Police had done this to keep him out of jail for the time being because he was only eighteen. What was he arrested for? Blowing up his garage with a pipe bomb while his mother was in the house. Upon further investigation, they found a stockpile of pipe bombs and firearms in his possession.

Adam was quiet in group therapy, but it became apparent that he was very angry. He talked about an instance of abuse when his father had tackled him onto the bed to get two more pipe bombs out of his hands which confused me because it seemed perfectly rational. He seemed to resent the charges against him because he claims he didn't know his mother would be home and how he should be moved to a lower security ward, even though our ward was about as low security as it gets. He also talked a lot about what he thought school shooters were like, how they were quiet kids, like him, and I eventually realized that he was a would-be school shooter.

The oddest part was that this didn't seem to affect our friendship at all. We still did our puzzle and didn't talk much and I never asked him about the bombs or the guns. He was just my puzzle friend. He was signed out early in the morning, before I woke up, near the end of the week for court. He never came back to the ward after that and none of us ever found out what happened to him. I remember being mad at him, but not for being a violent, angry criminal. I was mad because he left before our puzzle was finished and he never said good bye. It took me months after being out of the hospital to realize how strange this was. The hospital was a strange place, though. When I first got out, I told people that you "checked your ego and sharp objects at the door."

Lauren left the ward before me and I cried. I was perfectly fine with being there until she left; that was when I started to want to go home. I didn't even spend a whole ton of time with Lauren on the ward, we had very different things that we had to sort through. A good amount of people left the ward around the same time as Lauren and we got a whole set of new people. I didn't want a new roommate, but I had a few after she left. I never even learned their names because they were moved out of the ward after just one night. One of them talked to me a lot about cheeking pills, a way to avoid taking medication or stockpiling pills to trade. That was my first and only experience with someone who truly didn't want to get better.

Most people do want to get better, though. People who are leaving a mental hospital actually go to an intensive outpatient treatment program in a different area of the hospital called the partial hospitalization program. The program is usually about two weeks long and its sort of like a job. You go during the day, five days a week, and do group therapy every morning. The afternoons are set up a bit like school, with classes and activities to learn how to cope with different things. After that you move onto weekly therapy and so on, but you never really stop treatment.

When I left the ward, I almost cried. I had such mixed emotions about that place by the day I was discharged. I was and remain firmly convinced that the hospital saved my life, but, after a while, it seemed to suck that life back out of me. I was happy to leave the ward; seven days had felt like years when I finally stepped outside. A lot happened to me the months leading up to my hospitalization, but even more happened in those seven days I was there. I had found all these people, too many to name here, that I cared about and even loved, but the reality of the hospital is, if I truly wanted us to get better, to do well, that meant we'd never see each other again.

Other thoughts on my hospitalization:

Besides Claire, who was discharged soon after I arrived, and Adam, who was the silent, violent type, John was the only other teenager on the ward. He had been there for three weeks, I couldn't even imagine that, but he'd been ready to be released for about a week now. I mainly try to stay away from John because he made me feel guilty. He was nineteen and his father didn't think it was a good idea for him to go home. He thought he was too feminine, too weak, cried too much and just didn't want to live with him, but what made it even sadder to me was that his mother agreed with his father. I couldn't imagine a mother not wanting her child to come home.

John had just graduated high school, like me, and spent most of his time since in mental health crisis. He hadn't even had a chance to be an adult yet and he truly had nowhere to go, but the hospital wouldn't, couldn't release a patient without somewhere to go. His parents would come in early in the morning, like they didn't want anyone to see them there, and made plans to send him out of state. They had been calling distant relatives from all over the place, trying to find someone to take their mentally ill son. I couldn't imagine coming home from that strange new planet to a place I'd never been before.

Lauren's story was completely heartbreaking and came out slowly during her stay. She had a little sister who had suddenly gotten sick in mid-elementary school. She ended up not making it, which completely destroyed Lauren. Her mother was also the oldest of two sisters, with the younger of the two dying in childhood, which made her believe that it was something that somehow ran in her family. She wanted to have children, but knew, truly knew, that her second child would die young. I've never seen guilt like that in my life.

My world had shrunk into a small section of the building: my room, the hallway with the meds window carved into the wall, and the dayroom. My room looked like someone had tried to replicate a college dorm, but couldn't get it quite right. All the furniture was the same light, fake looking wood, but there were no doors on any of it. All of the drawers looked like little cubbies, completely exposing all of your belongings, which sat behind doors that didn't lock. The walls were a little too white and the windows were carefully high-up and small, as if someone would climb out of one and escape. It was a locked ward, after all.

The hallway was long and oddly wide and lined on one side with identical doors to identical rooms, though we never went in each other's. They tried hard to make the whole area less harsh, but the window with a little metal sliding door in front of it sort of ruined that look. There was a long, round desk that was blocked off from patients, but always had at least three nurses behind it. Down past the dayroom were what looked like payphones, six, lining the wall. There was no privacy, no separation between them, just a chair beside each of them. We never talked to anyone for very long because the phones were only on twice a day for about an hour and a half.

The dayroom was made up of three long tables arranged in a U directly across from the front desk. There was a mismatch of chairs at each of the tables, I took great pains to always sit in the same one. Another, much larger window sat in the corner and opened up every morning to give us our breakfasts. I had frozen waffles. Everyday. There were puzzles and colored pencils and coloring pages and blank paper and playing cards, just like seemed fitting in a mental hospital. There was also a TV in the dayroom, the only TV on the ward. I really expected it would play something calm or soothing, but it played "Nightline," a reality show following ambulances, cops, and firefighters. It could be gory and intense, but never soothing. To this day, that show somehow makes me feel calm.

I'm 20 Years Old

(Witten at age 20)

I'm 20 years old and mentally ill
I carved up my arms and missed classes and still
I graduated high school with two honor society cords
And three different college scholarship awards
I went to college more than two hours away
I was on time for class most every day
I went to therapy, took meds, did everything right
Then hid my panic from my roommate at night
I went to a party and left in tears
And struggled each day to fit in with my peers
College, high school, middle school, way back
I hid all my symptoms, I put on an act
What seemed most important to me
Was protecting what I could someday be
It mattered to me when we were playing with toys
All the way up to talking about boys
I tried and struggled to understand
And worked hard every day to belong in a land
That existed out there beyond my own mind
That everyone else seemed to so easily find
I went to prom with a family friend
And felt like I was going to die by the end
I tried to kill myself when I was still a teen
I really didn't understand what that would mean
One day I was studying psychology, moving forward
The next I'm back home in a psych ward
Overnight I went from the studier to the studied
I felt as if my whole identity was muddied

I did puzzles and slept in a room with no lock
But I felt my brain could finally dock
Here where my fears don't seem so absurd
Here where I could speak, be understood, be heard
I was in a safe little treatment bubble
But after a few days I began to have trouble
Living in my little self-contained world
While everything outside those walls un-furrowed
I spent Thanksgiving stuck in a place
Where it was hard to find a familiar face
I stayed inside the whole 7 days
The world in slow motion, stuck in a haze
When I left that place I had a feeling of glee
As if it had been years since I was last free
And now, over a year removed
I sometimes miss the hospital that proved
To be the perfect place for me to come
To escape where I was coming from
A place where I had everyone fooled
And I had my brain so tightly spooled
Around fears and things that weren't even real
That I thought existed, I thought I could feel
And I never expected that I would get caught
In the intricate lies that I had always sought
To pass off as my own reality
To feign what I thought was sanity
And still my mind can move a little too fast
And whispers of my symptoms will last
In my strange little mind for the rest of my days
And the big world out here is still a bit of a maze
That I must walk through, like I've always done
But I feel like in some way I have won
After all, I am standing here
Despite all my anxiety, my struggles, my fear

I am back at school and I have grown
And I know I don't have to do all of it alone
I'm still taking my meds and doing everything right
But now I sleep quite soundly at night
So I guess what I'm trying to say
Is I've won because I'm alive today.

Goodbye
(Written at age 21)

Who knows how long
I'll be sitting here just missing you
Singing the same breakup song
And not knowing what to do

You never left my side
But you were never really there
Something I had to hide
But I always knew you'd care

I'll say it again to be clear
You were only ever in my head
But you never brought fear
With anything that you said

It should've been terrible
I should've been out of my mind
It was more than bearable
You caught thoughts I couldn't find

You weren't safe to keep
Just living up there in my brain
Where you could creep
Quietly and drive me insane

You said you would never
Hurt me like that
But you don't stay the same forever
And you do more than chat

You can't tell me what to do
You can't tell me who to be
It was never up to you
It's always been up to me

You didn't want me to let you go
You tried to convince me
But I need to grow
And getting rid of you was key

It's been a week
Now it's been two
You can't speak
I have to be over you

Alone in my mind
(Written at age 21)

My brain runs fast
But now I find
I am at last
Alone in my mind

She was there
At first to guide
She seemed to care
To be on my side

She comforted me
When I got stressed
And helped me see
Only the best

I put her asleep
I gave her away
I couldn't keep
Hearing her each day

She took some time off
She went when I asked
But came back with a scoff
And anger not masked

Not who she used to be
With new things to do
She said you kill me
Now I kill you

I banished her
To the back of my head
She created a stir
But I ignored her instead

My brain runs fast
But now I find
I am at last
Alone in my mind

Tragedy Thief
(Written at age 21)

I didn't always understand, like everyone else,
The little things that seem to make up everything.
I didn't feel a glance, a shrug, a small change,
But I could always feel a tragedy.

I had no claim to the events that fell around me,
But I still collected all those I saw,
Like a little girl collecting sea shells at the beach
And taking what belonged to the ocean.

I stole the tears out of the eyes of the mourners
And painted them on my own face in the dark.
I found rocks to lie beneath
To match the weight on their chests.

I wrapped my hand around my heart
And squeezed until blood came through my fingers
Just as it would if your heart was really caught
In the tight vice of grief.

I dug myself a hole in the dark, damp earth
And hid in the lightless, cool shelter
As they plunged into the darkness
Of the crater opening beneath their feet.

I allowed myself to be taken back,
On the wild ride that is grief,
To my own times of suffering and loss,
As if they had happened only moments ago.

I drowned myself in news and stories
From the worst days of peoples' lives
And swam down into the dark
To lie there on the floor of despair.

I accepted compliments from others,
So empathetic, such a good heart,
But deep down I knew what I was.
I was nothing more than a tragedy thief.

Happy, Mayor of Crazy Town
(Written at age 21)

Around when I turned 21, I started to hear a voice named Josie. Josie was a nice voice at first. Named one of the names my parents considered naming me, she was a version of myself without OCD, autism, or anxiety. This was a new symptom for me. My psychiatrist said I was dissociating. I was so anxious that my brain had just separated that part out and made it into a whole new person. A whole new version of me. It was funny because I didn't even feel anxious. The other person, Josie, had taken all that over.

I started taking medicine to get rid of Josie and it worked at first. The problem was it made me extremely anxious. All of the anxiety that I had given to Josie was now back on my shoulders and it was really hard. Right when I was starting to get back to my feet, though, Josie came back. She wasn't so nice this time. She said nasty things to me and pretty much tried to ruin my day. I told my psychiatrist right away, but that didn't stop Josie from talking to me. She started to tell me to kill myself.

When Josie started to try to get me to commit suicide, it became clear that I would have to go inpatient again. I wasn't completely happy about the situation, but it was the situation I was in. At the emergency room, they had a hard time finding me a bed. They said that I could go to a hospital in the city, but I could go to the same hospital that I went to before if I waited until the next morning. I waited until the next morning.

After sleeping in a couch in the waiting room of the ER, I was pretty stiff, but happy that I could go somewhere familiar. I don't remember exactly how long the intake process took last time, I was pretty out of it, but it seemed to take forever this time. Forever was about three hours. I went back on to the same unit I was on before, but it was populated with a whole new cast of characters. A lot of the staff were the same, but there was no overlap in patients.

The first group therapy session I was in I made sure that I spoke first. I said exactly what I was thinking. I was mad. I did everything right. I didn't drink or smoke or do any drugs or party at all, I don't even drink caffeine. I took my meds every day, I went to therapy, and I was just starting to eat right and go to the gym. I did everything right and my symptoms were just throwing me curve balls every time I thought I was better. It felt good to say and it felt good that a professional was telling me that I was justified. It was just good to be allowed to be mad.

There was a girl in the hospital with me named Destiny and she was mad too. She was a different kind of mad, though. She would throw fits, screaming and yelling, she even flipped over a table. It broke. We both had autism so she thought we were the same, but we weren't. I wasn't mad like she was. My parents visited me twice a day and hers never visited the whole time I was there. I wonder if that was the difference.

I had a roommate who didn't last long on the unit. She was moved to a new unit after less than 24 hours because she was dual diagnoses. That means that she was detoxing from something too. She was a new mother. I saw more than one person detoxing off of whatever it was.

They could be some of the sweetest people in the world, but it didn't matter. They would still get angry and scream at staff when they were going through withdraw.

Josie was very mad at me for "trying to kill her" with medication and, honestly, I felt guilty about that too. That's when Happy's advice really helped me. He said I shouldn't think of it as having killed Josie, but rather as having put her to sleep. When I was able to control my guilt, I was able to see that Josie was always a part of me. I was able to reintegrate her into myself.

We had a movie night in the hospital. There were about six of us in one of the common rooms with popcorn, Oreos, Twizzlers, and lemonade. We watched "Rent Live," which wasn't actually live, but that didn't matter to us. We laughed and ate and had more fun than anyone should have in a mental hospital. I didn't make it to the end of the show, but I will always associate Rent with the hospital.

When I was finally released, I was happy to be out.Happy had been there longer than any of us so one of the other patients called him the Mayor. He was the mayor of crazy town. He was leaving the day after me, though. People come and go in the hospital pretty quickly. By now, there is a whole new cast of characters on the unit.

Cover art based on a drawing of my "OCD brain" that I made during
my 2016 hospitalization. All photos taken by me.

Printed in the United States
By Bookmasters